the solace of sound by fabian m thomas
ISBN 978-976-96594-4-5

Published by Independent VoYces Literary Works
Printed in the United States by Amazon/KDP

Other works by fabian m. thomas

- New Thought, New Words: a collection of gratitude verses, affirmations & spoken word
- Djembe
- Tribal Elements: (A Tribe Ting. Volume 1)

www.sankofaaf.com

the solace of sound

A collection of poetry and spoken word

acknowledgements

lost for words

almost

gratitude buck

heart full

butterflies aplenty

spirit and ancestors

in the midst

Tenky

Prof Mervyn Morris, editor extraordinaire

Lorna Goodison, you and your words reside in my heartland

Kwame Dawes, for first guidance at my first Calabash

Judith Falloon-Reid, sistren, fellow-writer, co-dreamer and now publisher.

Dedicated to my father,
Winston *'Tino'* Thomas

and my beloved
Leonie *'Miss Lee'* Forbes

CONTENTS

FORWARD BY LORNA GOODISON

These are the words of a gifted artiste and seeker who has come through by wild Grace into a place of radical wisdom, knowledge and understanding.

This anthology of spoken word poems is an offering consisting of spiritual ripe fruits he has gathered along the way; and they will nourish, cheer, console and delight all who receive them. They will help to bind-up the broken hearted and cause us all to laugh loud, loud and long. You are invited to tune-in to the words of this fabulous storyteller. You will receive something rare and you will be blessed.

Thanks Fabian!

seeking soul....

words

words
words
words
by which I am
ambushed
assaulted
assuaged
wayward
own way
words

one word
at a time
each word
added to a line
lines elongate into verses
verses expand into poems
poems that sometimes
morph into rants

words words words
sometimes hard to hear
better left unsaid
outward expression
of the happenings in my head
words to the living
words about the dead

words
mumbling
rumbling
stumbling
into being

words words
that will not wait

words words words
seeking soul
seeking sound
seeking solace
seeking
seeking
seeking

for Toni Morrison

Mother-Wordsmith,
you have shed your mortal casing
your wild, magnificent words rest
resplendent in the realm of the immortal now
like your soul

Your words
familiarized
estranged
mystified
normalized
invoked
cauterized
illumined

Your *Beloved*
played a chord in my heart
and soul
that I will never be able to un-hear
or forget
You altered my world
ignited my imagination

Mighty muse
You have left us physically
but you will never be gone,
inseparable from us
I am bound to you
tethered by the bounty of your luminous lyricism

Oh Miss Toni, what a legacy!
as we say in Jamaica
walk good, *Beloved*.

I see you, Jharrel
(for Jharrel Jerome)

You shone in *Moonlight*
Bolstered my conviction with *Mr. Mercedes*
I was unprepared for what came next:
When They See Us
You became
Inhabited Korey Wise's trauma
Projected it in lurid detail
Yet with such grace
Navigated his resurrection
As if it was your own
You blessed me with bearing witness
To an actor disappearing
Giving life
To another being
It was holy and haunting
Simultaneously
Rest, young-King
Heal, regroup
We await
Your next gift…

juju man
(for Orville Nelson & Howard Daly)

he heals
seeing subcutaneously
seizing sickness
reaching remedies
connected umbilically
medicine passing
through the cords
that are his fingers

his hands
anointed
kneading flesh
massaging muscles
with homemade herbs
to alleviate ailment
mint, oil
proportioned precisely
for each person-patient

he walks
onto wards
looking inward
offering solace
easing dis-ease
affirming renewal
as he heals

live
(for A.)

her wrists
this time
stepping up from
pills and rat poison
graduating
to self-mutilation
slit them
she slit them
but lived
lived again
again to journey
until the next trigger

she doesn't seem to see
what we see
her amazing beauty
which causes
breath to stop short
causes people
to stop short
of open-mouthed staring
staring at her
deep dark skin
her cool aura
flashing eyes
elongated neck
breasts like palaces
legs that go on forever
legs that propel
her as she
negotiates the universe
the peaks and valleys

of her life
life in prison
imprisonment
born of death
"why did my father die and leave me?"
a sentence
engendered by beauty
put her in a box
without trial
a box
constructed by other people's
lust
objectification
envy, insecurity and fear

unfair to this prisoner
shackled since 13
by rape
picked and devoured
before ripening
violated again
by her stepmother's demand
for silence
she silently
inhaled the smell
of shame
swallowed the bile
of blame
this ingestion
did not bloat her belly
but clouded her mind

how will she
let go
of the pain

of her past?
when will she
love herself
so she
can heal herself?
i'd like to put
a mantra in her mind:

live
you are blessed

live
you are beautiful

live
you are loved

live
you are a child of god

live
your ancestors demand
and deserve it

live
you are enough

live
you are whole

live
you are healed

live
live
live.......

Sisters
(for Sapphire)

She
American Dreamer
woman queen
seamstress
weaving prose and poetry
into tapestries
of flame
words, hard
soft, arrogant
unapologetic
resonate
dare me to listen
stretch
an umbilical cord
through space, time and gender
I catch my breath
my heart
swells full
blood boiling
sweat, fear
guilt
her eyes are sharp and bright
her voice
plaintive, painful
strangely familiar
hypnotic
I listen with
reverence
because I must

She
brown beautiful
writer-healer
emits sparks
that threaten to
blind me
but instead
open my eyes
I wonder
how it is
that she moves me
so deeply
with so little effort
daring me to hear
her song of survival
my ears quiver
but open
to stories of sapphires
wrenched from blue-black lives
psyches, throats
breasts, vaginas
I am the colour of disbelief
denial, horror
feel like an intruder
voyeur to the
murky, moist
menacing depths
of these journeys

I
relax, allow
her words
to erode my male security
the abuse
infects me

screaming
as I become a little girl
with whipped cream
semen, blood
shit on my lips
river of precious blood
I want to
gather her in my arms
hold her
until the pain stops
hold her
until the storm passes over
hold her
until
hold her
return to her
her childhood
her virginity
reconstruct the shattered
fragments
of her little-girl pelvis
bathe and balm her tortured anus
with my hands

She
tells truth like shrapnel
undresses herself
stands naked
exposed, healing
goddess risen
from the quagmire
I listen
love, believe
weep, laugh
wait

my chest relaxes
I sob
quietly now
my head throbs
I am floating
I am woman, girl
I am
my sister-self.

Sunni
(to Sunni Patterson)

You stand
Firm
Feet planted
Anchored
Bald head
Balled fists
Balls of fire
As eyes
You tilt your head
Pendulous earrings
Hanging from your lobes
Like love
Your lips drip
Drops of life
Word-elixirs
Trickle down
Ravaged throats
To harrowed hearts
Clearing clots
From atrium
To ventricle.

You raise rants to
Cauterize collective wounds
Stitch flayed flesh
Back into place
Reconnect ligaments ripped
From broken bones
Stretch shorn skin
Back over carcasses
Breathe life back
Into the bodies of dead children

Massage scalps
Braiding the hair
To cover head trauma.

And somehow
I know you
'We know this place'
You (re)kindle a flame
Long burning
Graft words onto my tongue
Anoint my head
With the oil of
Words from your womb
My cup runs over
To speak volumes
Luminously lyrical
Mother/father/sister/brother tongues.

Sunni
My dear sister
From the land of levees
Thank you
For being
For writing
For speaking
For singing
Catharsis
Exultant and thick
Heavy with harsh realities
Yet lightened by iridescent truth
Crafted with uncommon prowess
Spoken with unequivocal eloquence
Reverberating reverence
That rises
Then rests
In my soul.

altar

i
will not
take for granted
my freedom
my being
my life

i will
love myself
my ebony skin
nappy hair
full lips
my nose, eyes

i
will not
disrespect
my body-temple

this altar
is
sacred.

Ocean
(to Ocean Morisset)

you
shimmering expanse
like the earth-force
whose name you bear
effortlessly
with unabashed
openness
you offer forth
your liquid-luminescence
adjusting the aperture
of your life
allowing us
to see you
uninhibited
unmasked
eloquently exposed
snapshots
from your heart and soul
on the streets
at home
before and after
chemo
bald
bearded
catheterized
feverish
thermometer between
pursed lips
defiant, yet pliant
solid, but supple
beautiful
you

make words fail me
make me catch my breath
I am filled
with you
this man
I have never met
but feel as if
I know
I dive into the Ocean
of you
I become aware
of your warmth
your potent life-force
haitian-spirit
kindred-soul
my brother
across the caribbean sea
through cyberspace
I am touching
your face
laughing with you
basking in
the resonance of
your voice
watching you
with camera in hand
eyes and heart open
holding you
when you shiver
Ocean,
i see you
you are
whole
healed
complete

cancer-free
radiant
your resilient spirit
effusive warmth
unleashed
full force

and so it is.

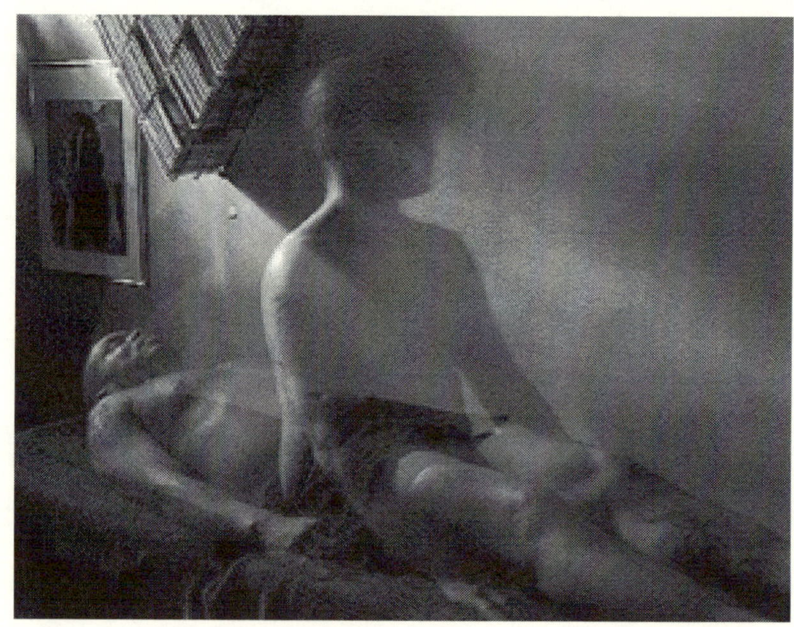

retreat/escape

recently
i realized
i have retreated
retreated into myself
sought refuge
in the folds
of my own flesh
ever expanding
caverns for me to
hide in

i have moved into
the house of loneliness
isolation
has seeped into my skin
poured into my pores
coloured my complexion
smothered my smile
hardened like calcium
under my nails
but understand this

i fill my void
with activity
wafts of warmth
flickers of friendship
sparks of sex
iotas of inclusion
temporary respites
that leave me unfulfilled

i have given notice
to isolation
stopped paying
loneliness' rent

i am going to love
my body
reshape it
for me
in my own time
and love it
love hard and strong
fuck a six-pack
happiness
and thinness
are not synonyms

i will only share
my heart with those who
want and deserve this gift
i am escaping

for Prof Baugh

It was the marvellous resonance
of your voice, and
the wisdom you imparted with it.

It was the grace-filled space
you allowed us to
bask in
be part of.
It is the timeless wonder
the luminous gift
you gave us, when
you wrote *It was the singing*.

it is your legacy
it is your life, Sir.

walk good, Prof...

sista erykah

u go girl
go on sista girl
go on & on diva
on & on & on & on
take us higher
deeper
2 the very heart
of the matter
laid bare
by the prophetic
healing tones
of your voice

a voice
brittle, full
sweet, bitter
honest, real
playful, angry
all & none
of the above
all at once
& not at all
universal
spectral
yours

mother billie smiling
over there
saying "god bless the child"
bless u chile
u've got your own
u child
nubian princess

your being
a blessing
your body
a temple
housing a spirit
ancient, wise
telling it
like it is
was
4ever shall be
amen!

baduizm…
missives emanating
from an old soul
but so new
fresh and refreshing
locks atop your head
a head
filled with
magical motifs
redolent riffs
succinct scats

sista erykah
sing sweet
swing low
tell the sweetness
of a sista's heart
expose the sinews
of a sista's strength
promote the pervasive
nature of a sista's pride
sing 'bout brothas & sistas
rimshots & apple trees

4 leaf clovers & afros
games & their other sides
lifetimes 2 come
take us to eve's bayou

just sing on
talk about it
go on
inspire
go on
preach
go on
teach
go on
heal
on&on&on&on
on&on&on&on
on&on&on&on
sista girl
spirit woman
child mother

erykah badu

for Whitney

Whitney, my sister
I wish you had chosen
differently
had lived your truth
unmuzzled
remembered who
and whose you were
exercised your power
rose above earthly angst

I am sorry
so many
thrived on your talent
fed on your pain
sank their fangs into
your unravelling
drank their fill
as you drowned

I celebrate
the wondrous gift that you were
defining, dominant siren
of a generation
thanks for so sweetly
adding to the soundtrack of my life
so often
you came into our lives
your light luminous
you warmed us
wooed us
sang our lives
loved us fiercely
we loved you back
flaws and all

Rest now diva
rest.

dancer-woman
(for Patsy Ricketts)

she
enters
the dancescape
lithe, fleet of foot
regal revelation
supple hands
eyes speaking volumes

back arched
arms raised
leg lifted
point
flex
attitude
arabesque
contract
breath
hold
release

she danced
told tales
embodied ancestral truths
bared her soul
from the soles of her feet
to the crown of her head
her body blessed those who bore witness
with narratives ancient
retold with exquisite grace
muse
we salute you
bless you

love you
we give thanks for the gift that you are
you have danced your way into our hearts
into the fabric of our lives
onto the palette that illustrates who we are
your name is indelibly inscribed

you are
elemental force of nature
dancer-woman
sweet-sister
mother-in-motion
standard-bearer
flash of the Spirit
earth-bound Holy Grail

we speak your name
with love
Patsy Ricketts.

legendary
(for John Legend)

lyrically lost
looking
longing
4 an oasis
clean crisp
crystal-clear
quencher
satisfying
the soul
with songs of real life
real love
real talent
beyond the ordinary
far removed from
flash-in-the-pan
penny operas
rehashed riffers
rip-offers
posers

searching
since
rachelle & rahsaan,
erykah & lauryn
jill & india
kina & kindred
vivian g & billy p
me'shell & maxwell
coming up
empty-handed
enter stage right
this brown-boy

soul-brother
music-man
writing
playing
singing
telling it
as if he has lived
many many lives
centuries
millennia
bringing
sweet
hip-hop, soul, r & b, jazz, gospel
pot pourri
of mantras
melodies
for our time
yet timeless
doing his own
thing
with traces of
influence
inheritance
of those B4
ray   donny
rance   stevie
peabo   luther
james   jeffrey
yet with
style, flair
delivery
deliciously his own
thank u
john
4 lifting us
raising the bar

inspiring song
poetry, prose
4 affirming
our lives
our hope
our love
our voice
with yours
soaring
as U
make your mark
blaze your trail
sing your songs
make your music
john
your name
your voice
your music
your magic
will
become

legend

L'ACADCO
(for Dr. L'Antoinette Osunide Stines)

we are
pocomania and pointe shoes
classical ballet and kumina
wi can
butterfly and willie bounce
do di tattie, worl dance, dutty wine but also
fouetté and gran battement
execute L'Antech, Horton, Graham

we are
the middle passage,
African diaspora
british-ruled
independent
brukins
jonkanoo
kum inna dis!

we are Jamaican
Ashanti
Cromanti
Taino
Carib
Oshun
Shango
downtown
uptown

We are L'ACADCO
a united Caribbean dance force!

i give thanks

Mother, Father
Everything....God
Everywhere
Evenly present
I give thanks always
All my days
For every single thing
In every song I sing

Just as David
Had all he needed
To fulfil his destiny
So it is with me
I've already got
My stones and slingshot
Ready to slay
Whatever stands
In my way

I give thanks
For your power
Accessible every hour
For your protection
For guiding my direction
I bask in the realization
That there is no separation
Just as the wave
Is inseparable from the sea
So it is with you and me

Mother, Father
Everything....God

Everywhere
Evenly present
I give thanks always
All my days
For every single thing
In every song I sing

seeking sound....

ascension

learning
growing
opening like a bud
blossoming like a flower
soaring bird-like
spirit-led
soul-fed
seeking
finding
truth
my Christ-self
holding fast
becoming
knowing
being

ascending

awake

a poem
woke me
up this morning
broke me open
wide awake.

armour

intransit
like me
between st. maarten
and st. kitts
lashes like windshield wipers
hovering above black-lined eyes
lifeless jet-black bang
resting against
her forehead
threatening
to intertwine with
remnants of
her eyebrows

face layered
pancake-mix thick
pouting lips
blood-red on top
bruise-black beneath
bulbous breasts
love handles encircling
protruding belly
all these, bound
girded & fettered
under a fluorescent
lime-green blouse
imprisoning
its captives

mannish hands
store-bought fingernails
garishly feminized
with nail polish
screaming baubles
and bashment bangles

sharp and sudden
tapering from waist
to ankles
a narrowing
defying balance
and support
then there were
her toes!
digital glory atop
battered, discoloured feet
pinky toe emerald green
next one white
next one purple
next one pink
big toe
talon-like
metallic green
with silver streaks
punctuated by
gaudy 'goodas' glitter
feet spilling out of
suffering sandals

eyes full
i wonder
what paths
which experiences
was it trauma
or euphoria
self-love or
internalized hate
or exaggerated pride
that caused her
to need
choose to
adorn herself
in this armour?

At 38

At 38
my wishes were
continued growth
the pursuit of excellence
lifelong learning and
being unafraid
to reinvent myself

I wanted to
remain committed to trying
to be the best me possible
to aim high,
be inspired and inspiring
humble, yet high-stepping
a trail-blazer
unafraid of being exceptional

I vowed
to tell the people I love
that I love them
repeatedly
to touch, hug
laugh and play with
uplift and transform
them with my love and life force
to thank them for being in my life

I said
I'd never forget who I was or
where I was coming from
that I'd grasp my magnificent destiny
with both hands
and not let go
I'd be ready for life's challenges
unashamed of the gift
of my tears

attack

the summoned onlookers said nothing

acidic accusations
verbal venom
shredded my name
sullied my reputation
pain washed over me in waves

there was silence

the onslaught continued
phone calls with prejudice
covert consultations
clouded conclusions
jagged judgment
ripped into my gut
gavelled my head
to a bloody pulp

the familiar speechless jurors bore witness

the bloodletting & silence crescendoed
i almost lost consciousness
but wrenched my flesh free
his forked tongue stung
i gathered the torn shreds
of my skin
tourniqueted my soul
resuscitated my spirit
sutured my pride

in the deafening silence...
....i cried:

rabid lies cannot
define
defile
derail me
i know who i am
tongues sting and burn
but will not deform
revived
strengthened
resolved
i press on
wounded
but healing
bruised & battered
but not broken
this too shall pass..

...i embrace the silence

i wonder
(for a rising star)

i wonder
if they paused
before
they pressed the button
to stop the press
to set in motion
images and words
that would unhinge your life
rip off the door
leaving the innards
exposed and raw

i wonder
if you imagined
that a friend
or at least
someone you trusted
would 'out' you
in bilious detail
try to darken
your rising star

i wonder
if they gathered
in a frenzied rush
to suss
salivate
and snicker
as they plotted

spied
pretended to be
journalists

i wonder
if media gurus
talk show hosts
press or media association
academia
non-gay cabinet
will say something
anything
speak up
make a statement
about common decency

i wonder
when the tension
in my chest and stomach
will ease
i wonder
when the heteroterrorism
fuckery
will end
when will we mean
what we say
when we sing:
"One Love, One Heart"?

jamrock

wi laugh loud
go hard
dweet sweet
ramp rough
lick hot
dance wid screw face
a nation in trauma
acting as if there are
no problems.

abeng in Beijing

Battle-ready
in black, green and gold
warrior-runner
Usain bolted
ahead of the world
from Sherwood Content, Trelawny
this 6′ 5″ sprint anomaly
stamped his sunshine-bred supremacy
shattering red, white & blue ascendancy
it was bound to spark controversy
an some almshouse chat from the IOC
oh i see
the real issue is
how dare he?
dis lickle black bwoy
from di land of wood & wata
him too outta arda
now dem waan test wi yam an cassava

Beating his chest
like a kumina drum
Usain
took it to dem
then danced barefoot
while the world watched
he danced for us
in a language they did not understand
like the abeng of old
they could not decode
bad min a go meck
some a dem explode
oh say can you see?

dem cyan chat to wi
did you see the untied lace?
dem a go tiyad fi si usain face
hol' on, my bad
let me correct what i said:
dem a ago tiyad fi si
di back a Usain head!

YELE!

Mother Earth rumbled
In response
To the words
Heaped upon you
Epithets added
As if part of your name
'poorest nation'
'cursed by God'
'voodoo capital'
'satan worshippers'

She churned
Remembering the forgotten
Boukman and L'Ouverture
1st independent nation in Latin America
Bondage repugnant
Irritant to your spirit
Toxin rejected by your blood
You, punished with two Duvaliers
Tonton Macoute
100 years of reparations to France

She coughed
Choking on injustice
Aftermath of embargos and deforestation
Gasoline neckties stuck in her craw
She heaved
Shattering limbs
Took a deep breath
Inhaling buildings
Leveling the land
Belching off the bile

Mother Earth shifted
When she settled
The smell of death
Hung thick everywhere
Then hope rose resolute
Memories were jogged
The indefatigable Haitian spirit
Sprang up from amidst the rubble
And danced, shouting
Yele!

11, 14, 17 days
Buried, yet alive
We will not go quietly into the night!
With amputated limbs
Broken hearts and homes
We will not give up!
Do you know who we are?
Egalite! 1st black republic in the world
Yele! We are Haiti!
We shall rise again!

Known by a few names, Le Marron Inconnu de Saint-Domingue (shortened as Le Marron Inconnu), Le Negre Marron and Nèg Mawon (pronunciation in Haitian Kréyol), is the bronze sculpture depicting a man, clad only in torn shorts, kneeling on his right leg. His left leg is outstretched behind him, a broken iron chain lays on the ground around his left foot. He arches his torso back as he holds a conch shell to his lips with his left hand, tilting his head upward. His right hand holds a machete at the ground. Commissioned by the Duvalier government, the statue was created to commemorate the abolition of slavery in Haiti by Albert Mangonès and completed in 1967.

middle passage

did the dolphins know
merrily swimming astern
the hell in the hold?

we still are…

We were
kings & queens
before we were
enslaved

We
still are.

two score an ten

Two-score an ten
Remembering when
Jamaica weaned herself

Mi know she predate di actual day
By lickle more dan 270 years
But I imagine
Nanny unhinging her jaw
Reaching inside her chest
Grasping the Jamaican flag
Pulling it through her throat
Unfurled, perfect
Snapping her mandible back in place
I see her
Holding our flag high above her wrapped head
Silently mouthing the word: FREE
And it echoing across the island
To the top of Blue Mountain peak
Rolling down into all the rivers
Making the water sweet, crystal-clear

Two-score an ten
Half a century of Independence
Wid varying degrees of vengeance
'bout two hundred years after
Cat-o-nines shredded brown flesh
Then salt applied for good measure
When racks stretched & flayed limbs
Wracking dark bodies with agony
A time of customary bloodletting
Blood, shed
Like water
Reddening earth and air

In my head
From spots where
Droplets gushed
Flowers sprang up, hungrily
Plasma-red bulbous blossoms
Emitting pungent perfume
Pervading the air
Those who inhaled it
Became truculent
Insisting on
Ravenous for
Freedom
To be Independent

Two-score an ten
Between now an den
This black-green-gold nation state
Has spawned
The most influential artist of the Millennium
Jamaica
Mothered
The Father of Black Consciousness
And forgotten him
I pledge my heart forever
Bred, fed and unleashed
To di werl
The fastest man on the planet
Jamaica
We have witnessed the days of Dudus
To serve with humble pride
Dese last days it look like
More skin a bleach now dan clothes
Jamaica
But still
Jamaica

We rise, soaring
Like Captain Barrington Irving Jr.
Jamaica, Land We Love

Ready fi di nex'
Two-score an ten.

land we love!
(for Franklyn 'Chappie' St. Juste)

its size belying its impact...
surpassing over-simplification
bigger than
the mantle of sun, sea and sand
proudly, offering instead
inimitable, diverse
sensory delights
aplenty

here
ancient recipes, passed down
picquant spices commingle with
complementary fireside companions
grown, bred in this place
that feed and power legs
that go on to dominate tracks
and fields worldwide...

from this place
listen!
aural delights of drum and bass
waft sweetly through the air
to stages, studios, airwaves
far and wide
"pull up selecta...
...wheel an come again!"

yah so
proud originations
of rastafari
overstanding and livity
have and continue

to bless planet earth
give thanks!

lickle, but tallawah
island-nation
land of wood and water
swag tun up ‘til it buck
from jerk to fricassee
Wint to Bolt
Louise to Lorna
Bob to Beenie
Merlene to Shelly-Ann
from Jamaica
to di werl!

no one helped him

the iron pipe swung downwards
the boy's head got in its way
"batty bwoy!"
a knife made its mark
his flesh gave way
"chi chi man"
timberlands lent a hand
these boots are made for walking...on your face
"homo!"

no one helped him
when the first insult was hurled his way
"fish!!"
when the first bottle was broken
on his head
"boom bye bye inna batty bwoy 'ead!"
when he fell to his knees
as if praying
"let him who is without sin...."
no one helped him.

no one helped him
as his brothers surrounded him
for this death ritual
hate gleaming in their eyes
"from dem a par inna chi chi man cyar..."
in spite of his screams
"....bring di fiya meck wi bun dem!"
no one stepped in pleading foul play
there were eight of them, only one of him.

no one helped him
when he ran through the streets
gasping for breath
they deafened their ears to his cry for help
averted their eyes
his blood spattering the pavement
he tried to slow its flow
with his hands
but he only had two.

no one cared that he could hear
his own heart pounding
threatening to free itself
from the prison of his chest
that he could feel his life-force ebbing
that he knew he was dying
that he had never really loved a man
or been loved by one
the boy was still a virgin.

no christian soldiers came marching
even though he lay bleeding
only 17 years old
dying in the street
hands reaching out for help
his eyes rolling back in his head
he died
alone.

no one helped him.

this snap's for you!!

for all
heterofanatic homophobes
who try to
diminish. dismiss, deny, degrade
my life
my existence
my humanity

for all
frenzied frothy-mouthed bible thumpers
who beat me
about the head and shoulders
with the gospel
damning me to hell
with fervour

for all
media marionettes
who scurry
like roaches
to negate our demise
make aids a real issue
with a wave of their new found 'magic' wand

for all of the above
and then some
i will sing and shout
until your eardrums shatter
your eyes pop
and your mouths gape
i will write words of fire

i want to let you know
we're going to survive
be happy and make happy
love and be loved
no matter what you do
let's just say
this snap's for you!!

bad man

bad man nuh wash
bad man nuh cook
bad man defen cash
bad man nuh read book

bad man nuh giggle
bad man nuh ramp
bad man nuh walk an wiggle
no punk cyaan inna bad man camp

bad man nuh fraid
bad man nuh cry
bad man nuh parade
wid no informa guy

bad man a di bes
bad man rule fram coas to coas
if a bwoy waan come tes
bad man tun im inna ghos

it gwine be a good-lickle while
before good man start run tings again
bad man a di lates style
run go tell yuh fren

harvest

the fruit
bruised
battered
bulging with blight
fell heavily
from the tree

he fell
as if from the air
into the midst
of their lives
into their arms
onto their loins

putrid nectar
spurted
squirted
splashed with spite
onto their faces
on their tongues

and all were
tainted
tarnished
tempted to touch
underneath
the tree

as he decays
they fold their arms
wash their faces
lick their lips
waiting
wondering
watching wide-eyed
for the next
forbidden fruit
to fall

Celie's reply

"He jus climb on toppa me and do his business"
her words ring
like a slap
in my ears
"Do his business? Why Miss Celie, you make it soun
like he going to the toilet on you!"
"Dat's what it feel like…"
my eyes water
as if from the jolt
of a punch
and i feel it
being drawn out of me
into words
but this birthing feels different
"Why Miss Celie, what us gon do?"
not polite
no controlled correctness
Miss Celie, what you gon do?
What you gon do, what you gon do?

Chile…..
i's gon cook
plenty and often
all his favourites
hot water cornbread
batter better with my spit
chitlins and hot sauce
with some of the shit left in 'em
peach cobbler sweetened
with ground up glass
ha….yes suh
that'll sure nuff
tear up that ass!

Baby, i's gon step an' fetch it
play nice
real nice
act dumb
smile wide
wide as the slash
i'm gon put
'cross his cussed no-good neck!

Don't be looking at me
like that chile
all sanctified and siditty
you asked me what i's gon do
and i told ya
now leave me be
i got's me some cooking to do!

Dear Nyekachi

Dear Nyekachi
tank yuh!
for being our surrogate
at miss worl'
thank you
for being our joy erupting
and encircling Toni-Ann
for covering her
with (y)our genuine love & support
thank you
for standing in the gap
across the Caribbean
an odda seas
for being sista-queen
fren an fambly
wi si yuh
your heart, visible
your light bright
like stadium bulb
big up yuhself
yuh…a goodaz.

p.s. you are now an honorary Jamaican!
come visit soon
so wi can love
an hug yuh up!
signed
Jamaica.

the love that makes us one

One word
Four letters
One four-letter word
Love
The simplicity of its sound
Masking its power
Pure
Potent

If we
Look beyond the physical veil
Use our spiritual vision
Which denies and defies
Our leanings towards
Human short-sightedness
We will
See

See
Like Neytiri in Avatar
When she said to her father
"I see you"
See
Beyond the physical
Beyond flesh
Beyond man-made
And ardently reinforced
Separations
Labels
Boxes
And bias

Love is not a thing
Love is THE thing
All powerful
The ultimate
Love my people
Is the final frontier
No need for the ensign to make it so
No need for Scotty to beam us up
Baby, we are already here!
Baby love, wi deh yah

Ubuntu
I am, because we are

Here's the thing
Mother/Father/Everything/God
Is everywhere
Evenly present
And since God is Love
Love is also
Everywhere
Evenly present
Love is
Above us
Below us
All around us
And more importantly
In us
We are love
Cut from its wondrous fabric
We are love walking
We are inextricably connected
And in our connection
This love connection
There is immense power

Light
Healing
Transformation
Joy

But who are we?
Why are we here?
We are here for greatness
For Love
To love
We stand on the shoulders of folks
Who went through some stuff
Endured, so we could be here
My question to you is: "What are you doing with
your survival?

I see you my sister
My brother
The divine in me
Sees, acknowledges
Celebrates the divine in you
I am you
You are me
We are one
Inseparable
Intimately linked
Linked by
Love

The love that makes us one

seeking solace....

baptism

cold water
against his hot skin
liquid hate
sears his pride
icy disapproval hardens
sending stigma like
shards into his heart
sharp intake of breath
acrid dust
fills his throat
he turns to his baptizers
his friends turn in sync
"i'm ok"
he wheezes
he keeps walking
choking on rage

later
hand holding
and hugs
soothe the sting
of shame
a change of shirt
warms the chill
of disrespect
love unconditional
slows his racing heartbeat
reality rushes in
his nerves settle
tears recede
vision sharpens
waiting for the blessing
from this baptism

forgetting

i am forgetting
what it feels like
to feel breathless
because someone is
breathing close to me
the delicious delight
of a dinner date
the flash of an uncontrollable smile
dancing across my face
prompted by a 'just because' gift
the unbridled giggle unleashed
by a silly sweet compliment
the skin-deep glowing warmth
of a sudden touch
the dizzying heady
commingling of cologne
and natural odour, not my own
the immeasurable pause
after a real kiss
moments of stillness
together
passing nations from my mouth
to another's ear
and the favour being returned
the quickening
and slowing
of steps and stride
that happens instinctively
when walking in duet
the holding of hands
cupping of faces
the wonder of watching
another sleep

and feeling love deepen
with each snore
the completeness of being
one and whole
with an equal

i am
forgetting....

Allen

i miss u
love u
more
than when our lives were intertwined

i wrestle
with the reality
of time
space
distance
between us
like a wall
shutting out the light

sometimes i cry
but mostly
i just miss u
love u
remember u
hold u
close

new year's resolution

i have realized that i need to regroup
retrace my steps
reconnect with my true friends
i no longer long to be accepted into
circles where i do not fit
i stop wasting hopes and invitations
on so-called colleagues and supporters
who don't show up
i no longer wait
to lose this weight
really feel comfortable in my skin
i unfetter my spirit
always stay connected
with the real friends
with whom i have been blessed
hold them close always
open my heart
let light in and out
open my mouth
sing, laugh, cry, speak
tell it
talk di tings
i am
bold, extraordinary and unapologetically successful
live out loud
laugh a lot
love fiercely and
dance often!

enter

enter me

walk around
feel my energy
see yourself here
inside

my walls will hold you
protect
enfold you
keep you safe

slip in between my layers
learn my innermost secrets
colour me yours

find your favourite spot
play in me
let your laughter echo within
wash me with your tears

fill me up
move into me

fitna…

i'm fitna
git close
so close
yo smell's
gon' fill me up
i'm fitna
taste yo sweet
sweat with ma tongue

i wanna git
close
so close
i'm gon'
be able to
feel you breathe
in
out
so close
we gon'
breathe together
out
in

i'm fitna
let you inside my
heart
under my
skin
all up an
roun my
innermost places
everywhere
then

i'm gon'
return the favour

i'm fitna
love you big
bold
fitna
let you love
me loud
long

fitna……

love you in stereo

i want
to love you in stereo
in surround-sound

i want to
revel
as our hearts beat
in tandem
my love
a song
sweet, strong
the notes
sure, long

i want
to inhale the smell of you
to taste your sweat, sweet
from the crown of your head
to the soles of your feet

i want to
celebrate
your presence
on the planet
hug, hold you
for a moment
or two

i want
to love you in stereo
in surround-sound

ebb & flow

point pressing hard
bruising me
trying to right
his soul
write wrongs
that only
he
sole witness
can express
lifeline laid out
on lifeless lines
languid markings
etched in careful
cursive precision
pressing against me
documenting angst
unrelenting emptiness
flooding
filling
my surface
with slow
painful certainty
inky deluge
spilling onto me
faltering
momentarily
i flutter
anticipating conclusion
instead
a pause

unexpected moisture
then finally
the flow ebbs into
silence

paper cut

flapping furiously upwards
the sheet of paper fluttered towards freedom
he grabbed it
wound the source of animation shut
then sucked where the spiteful sheet
had cut him

staring at the wound
steering with one hand
the road loomed up at him
the sun was mercenary
traffic like a knife slowly slicing skin

now slightly crumpled, the paper arrests his
attention
silently screaming its contents
at the next stoplight he reads the words on the
paper....again
then he folds it tightly neatly
sealing locking quieting the truth
and puts it in his shirt pocket

ten years had led to this journey
circuitous route to a place
where trials, laughter, good & bad times
had inextricably woven a friendship
from the threads of four distinct lives

precarious right turn taking him
too close to his destination
he decelerates, presses the pedal
the corners of the folded note

prick his flesh
pressing against him heavily

he drives past the gate again
turning right, then right again
then through the gate
his pocket sagging
into the house where two others wait
to share this weight
eyes bearing unspoken greetings
he unfolds the muted note
gives voice to its contents
the note falls free
landing beside the empty chair.

dear buju

dear buju
this started as a rant
your release
conflicted me
sycophant tweets
tumult of posts
gleeful crowds at airport
welcome fit for a hero
me adamant
I will not hail you as hero
excitedly
herald your return
mundane
matter of fact
done by myriads
who serve time
for deeds done
what warrants
this exuberance?
di same knife weh stick goat
clearly naah stick sheep
is such celebratory adoration
the entitlement of every 'outmate'?
or are you, now degreed
special?
is farrin conviction
what makes the difference?

I was insistent
the pain you caused
was too much
your venom-laced tongue
had cut too deep
with all that is known

there are stories untold
I could not see you
as blameless prodigal
mi naah kill no fatted calf!

I do not dismiss
the mark you have made
on our soundscape
I wonder, in fact
what word-sound
you, newly unmuzzled
will voice
but I cannot masquerade
'til Shiloh or not
with you in the role of messiah
it is still fresh
the ink from your poisonous
15-year old self
injurious mantra
anthem of hate
gifted to the world
with no return policy
force-fed to those
whose lives you sought to end
Boom
their skin torn
Bye
bones broken
Bye
blood spilt
on uneasy roads
fraught with danger

then I saw him
that boy
belching up

phobia he was fed
rancid and razor-sharp
I became present to
his victimization
by the village
that should have
shed light
but instead
struck the match
fanned the flicker
to a blaze
that seared the world
as it lined pockets
I realize
pain had compromised memory
obscured a truth
you had disavowed
allegiance to that tune
acknowledged the trauma
it inflicted
committed to no longer
give it
voice

gargamel
I wish you well
shrugging off the shroud
I had sewn myself into
embracing this
new paradigm
in which
I forgive you
and in so doing
free myself
making space
for a new narrative.

healing

come
to the water
and i will
hold you
bathe
your embattled body
wash your bludgeoned spirit
splash healing droplets
on your face
its beauty marred
sores left
by curse word venom
take my tongue
to these wounds
cleanse them
lance them
drain the pus

come to the water
your breath
fetid
with garroted truths
you fear to tell
and i will kiss you
my lips
engulf
you whole
my saliva
balm
to cancerous cankers
loosen your tongue
give you
voice

to affirm your life
set you to singing

come to the water
touch
my body
an exposed nerve
your hands
massage my insides
extract gangrene
from my veins
left by
hypodermic
phobias, hate
and derision
apathy
fair-weather
friends and family

come to the water
let us
prepare potions
spiritual elixirs
pride tonics
find others
bodies broken
souls shattered
eyes put out
spirits splintered
lead them
to the water
to bathe in love
and be healed.

Royal & Cora

He
extended his hand
to her
across the chasm
of his remorse
her shame
collective trauma
centuries old
personal pain
overwhelmingly present

He extended
his hand to her
and she
took it.

bredren

He looks at him
He holds his gaze
Something palpable, familiar
Brotherly, flows from one
to the other
He says "Come here"
He does so
He hugs him, tightly
He reciprocates, fully
Something passes
between them
Something like light
Something like healing
Something like
Love.

LAST NIGHT, I DANCED

last night, i danced.
i almost never do.
i am usually far too self-conscious
or tired
or at home.
but at Adodi, i dance.

here
we dance
our connection,
we dance
our love,
we dance
our healing,
we dance
as if no one is watching.

we dance
as if our ankles,
knees and thighs
will not ache in the aftermath.

we dance
beyond
barriers
despite
body type
regardless
of age
because
we are one.

we dance
with audacity.

we dance for the living
and the ibaye

we dance because
this space is sacred.
ashe!

last night
i danced.

(Adodi Retreat 2018)

Reggie asked, "Who will shed tears for the baby doves?"

we can, no
must
cry, wail, moan
laugh, sing,
scream

tell these same-gender loving
and transgender stories
though they bruise our hearts

we must speak
for those whose tongues
have been slashed at the root
stand, dance for those who have been limbed
from thigh to ankle

sing for those whose songs
have been ripped from their throats
we must be the wind for the fledgings
trying to flex their wings

we must bear them up
hold them close
dry their tears
feed them
dip them in pools
of love and light
thicken their delicate skin
teach them to soar

tell them
show them

they are loved
speak life to them
teach them
to survive.

In memory of

Dwayne Jones (16)
Carl Joseph Walker-Hoover (11)
Jaheem Herrera (11)
Tyler Clementi (18)
Seth Walsh (13)
Billy Lucas (15)
Asher Brown (13)
Zach Harrington (19)
Aiyisha Hassan (19)
Nokia Cowan
Victor Jarrett (26)
Sakia Gunn (15)
Matthew Sheperd (21)
Raymond Chase (19)
Mosey Diaz
Victoria Carmen White (28)
Arthur Downey (27)
Joseph Jefferson (26)
Nigel Shelby (15)

...and the countless other same-gender loving and non-binary youth, whose names I do not know, who took their own lives or had their lives ended because of who they were...

(strange) fruit

woman-born
man-child
pre-destined
to yearn
for others
like himself

to pick
eat
suck
forbidden
fruit

to hold
hands
like his own

seek
spirit-connection
with souls
like his

kiss
kindred lips

find peace.

mother
(for Mommy aka Theresa 'Terry' Thomas)

she

gives succour
offering sustenance

seemingly sure
through the uncertain

serene & tempestuous
silent & stentorian
(often simultaneously)

she is
safety, in the face of danger
be it sweet or sour

she stays.

closure

do not
expect
apologies
closure
from others
it may never come

forgive them
free yourself
close that door
suture the wound
let healing
begin…

survivors

we shall
overcome shame
no longer hide
stand naked
in our authentic truth
give voice
to our stories
because we
survived

tears

tears
    a gift
  salty remedy
healing wounds

      balm

let them
        flow

Secret Garden

Stone monument shouts
the names of silent children
as giggling ghosts play

The Secret Garden is a monument to Jamaica's slain children, at the intersection of Church and Tower streets, in downtown Kingston. Designed by sculptor, Paul Napier, it bears the names of approximately 450 of Jamaica's children who have been the victims of crime and violence and sits in a surrounding park.

inspirations

L'ACADCO (for Dr. L'Antoinette Osunide Stines)
L'ACADCO: A United Caribbean Dance Force is one of Jamaica's renown dance companies. Founder and Artistic Director, L'Antoinette Stines moved back to her homeland Jamaica in 1982 and has since then spearheaded the revolutionary fusion of rich Caribbean folklore with contemporary themes in an original and distinctive language/technique called L'Antech

Sunni (to Sunni Patterson)
Sunni Patterson is a poet and spoken word performer from New Orleans. I first experienced her on Def Poetry Jam, it profoundly changed my perception of and appreciation for spoken word performance.

Ocean (to Ocean Morisset)
Ocean Morisset is a published and award-winning photographer, visual storyteller and cancer survivor. We moved in similar circles, but never met while I lived in NYC. We connected years later on Facebook. I'm glad we did!

I see you, Jharrel
Jharrel Jerome is an American actor who leapt onto my radar in his film debut in Moonlight. He turned things up several notches with his stunning portrayal of Korey Wise in Ava DuVernay's Netflix miniseries When They See Us, which earned him the Primetime Emmy Award for Outstanding Lead Actor in a Limited Series or Movie. He continues to impress and inspire me.

for Prof Baugh
Prof Edward Baugh was a poet, biographer, and leading scholar of postcolonial Caribbean poetry. He was one of my Literature lecturers during my B.A. pursuit at the University of the West Indies. He impacted me greatly.

dancer-woman (for Patsy Ricketts)
Patricia 'Patsy' Ricketts was a principal dancer with the National Dance Theatre Company of Jamaica. She trained at Martha Graham School of Dance and was one of the founding members of Dance Theatre of Harlem. In 2014, she received the Order of Distinction, one of Jamaica's highest honours. I will always be fascinated by the magic of her hands and arms.

sisters (for Sapphire) Ramona 'Sapphire' Lofton is the author of Push (later converted to the screenplay and film, Precious), American Dreams, The Kid, and Black Wings & Blind Angels. My unsuspecting attendance at a reading from her American Dreams collection jolted me into a different level of writing viscerally.

land we love! (for Franklyn 'Chappie' St. Juste) 'Chappie' came into my life while I was an undergrad student at Carimac, UWI Mona. We later became colleagues. Our most memorable and significant collaboration was on the documentary *Sugar: Recycling Sweetness & Power* (which Chappie recommended me for as scriptwriter). One of our many pre-production sessions inspired me to write this poem. I am grateful I was able to share it with him before he left us.

Dear Nyekachi
Nyekachi Douglas is Miss World Africa / Most Beautiful Girl in Nigeria 2019/2020, as well as a Public Health student. Her unabashed delight and celebration when Miss Jamaica Toni-Ann Singh was announced as Miss World in 2019 went viral and was a joy to behold.

Royal and Cora
Royal and Cora are characters from the Golden Globe award-winning television series, created and directed by Barry Jenkins. Amidst the harrowing landscape he navigated, I found their brief relationship particularly poignant.

LAST NIGHT I DANCED
ADODI is a US-based intergenerational organization that offers affirming experiences and loving gatherings to foster emotional, physical and spiritual well-being for Same-Gender attracted Men of African descent.

IMAGE CREDITS

Cover Photo: Judith Falloon-Reid. Used with permission

1. Me an Miss Lorna. Photo by fabian m. thomas (foreword)
2. Photo of fabian m thomas taken by Hugh Wright for fabian m. thomas (Seeking Soul page)
3. Ocean (to Ocean Morisset) Photo by Ocean Morisset. Used with permission. (page 18)
4. Photo of fabian m thomas taken by Zaudspace for fabian m. thomas (page 34)
5. Le Negre Marron. Photo by Steeve Laguerre for fabian m thomas. (page 49)
5. Cacti. Photo by Michael Chambers. Used with permission (page 62)
6. Photo of fabian m thomas taken by Hugh Wright for fabian m. thomas (page 69)
7. Sentinel. Photo by Michael Chambers. Used with permission (page 87)
8. Adodi logo. Used with permission (page 91)
9. Secret Garden sculpture. Photo by Donette Zacca for fabian m thomas. (page 98)

ABOUT THE AUTHOR

fabian m thomas is a Calabash Writers Workshop Fellow. He has previously been published in Other Countries Press' (NYC) Sojourner: Black Gay Voices in the Age of AIDS (1993), Gents, Bad Boys & Barbarians: New Gay Male Poetry (Alyson Books, 1995), Fighting Words: Personal Essays by Black Gay Men (Harper Collins Publishers, 1999), Chroma: A Queer Literary Journal: Foreigners (Issue #3, August 2005), So Much Things To Say, 100 Calabash Poets (Akashic Books/ Calabash International Literary Trust, February 2010), The Caribbean Writer, Volumes 24, 25, 28 and 34, as well as Jubilation! (Peepal Tree Press, September 2012).

In addition to being awarded gold and bronze medals for Poetry in the Jamaica Cultural Development Commission's 2010 National Creative Writing Competition, fabian has also won the 2011 Charlotte & Isidor Paiewonsky Prize from The Caribbean Writer for first time publication, of his poem No One Helped Him, in Volume 24.

In 2018, fabian launched his first self-published book entitled New Thought, New Words, a collection of gratitude verses, affirmations and spoken word. His first children's book (illustrated) Djembe was released in February 2022 and Tribal

Elements (A Tribe Ting, Volume 1), a chapbook of original writings by members of his performing arts collective Tribe Sankofa was launched on April 23, 2022 as part of the collective's 10th Anniversary celebrations.

His short story Love, like a Bombay mango was long-listed for the 2021 Brooklyn Caribbean Literary Festival's Elizabeth Nunez Prize for Writers in the Caribbean.

fabian is also a Trainer/Facilitator, Adjunct Lecturer, Performing Arts Specialist and a Life, Corporate and Creative Coach.